FANS FROM THE FITZWILLIAM

A selection from the Messel-Rosse
collection
The Fitzwilliam Museum, Cambridge

Introduction and captions
by Nancy Armstrong

with R. A. Crighton and J. E. Poole.

Photographs by Andrew Morris
Designed by Tina Dutton
Production Services by Book Production Consultants,
Cambridge.
Origination by Cambridge Litho
Printed and bound by Foister and Jagg Ltd.
Typeset by Wenden Typesetting Services Ltd.

©Fitzwilliam Museum, Cambridge 1985

ISBN 0 904454 19 3

Published by Fitzwilliam Museum Enterprises Ltd.,
Trumpington Street, Cambridge CB2 1RB

Front Cover: Japan: Wide-ended Folding Fan
(Suehiro ogi) and associated wrapper, decorated
with "phoenix" and paulownia, wrapper with
peacock feathers and peony. Kano school. Fan:
paper, colours on gold. Wrapper: colour print from
woodblocks. 19th century.
Back Cover: The Messel Feather Fan. English or
Dutch, 17th century.

— BIBLIOGRAPHY —

Alexander, Hélène *Fans*, London, 1984.

Armstrong, Nancy *A Collector's History of Fans*, London, 1974.

Armstrong, Nancy *The Book of Fans*, Colour Library International 1978, London and New York.

Armstrong, Nancy *Fans*, London, 1984.

Crossman, Carl *The China Trade*, Princeton, 1972. Chapter 11, Fans.

Cust, Lionel *Catalogue of the Collection of Fans and Fan-Leaves presented to the Trustees of the British Museum by the Lady Charlotte Schreiber*, London, 1883.

Fan Circle International *Bulletins*, 1975-85.

Fan Circle International and Art Gallery & Museum Brighton *Fans and the Grand Tour*, catalogue of an exhibition, 2nd November, 1984-5th January, 1985.

Fan Circle International and The Victoria & Albert Museum *Fans from the East*, London (Debrett's Peerage), 1978.

Green, Bertha de Vere *A Collector's Guide to Fans over the Ages*, Muller, London, 1975.

Hay, John 'Chinese Fan Painting' in *Chinese Painting and the Decorative Style*, ed. Margaret Medley, London, Perceval David Foundation of Chinese Art, 1975.

Hughes, Therle 'Fantasy in Plume and Parchment, European Fans from the Leonard Messel Collection', *Country Life*, 8th June, 1972, pp. 1455-1458.

'Storm Dragons and Plum Blossom. Oriental Fans in the Leonard Messel Collection', *Country Life*, 15th June, 1972, pp. 1539-1541.

Impey, Oliver   *Chinoiserie: The Impact of Oriental Styles on Western Art and Decoration*, London, 1977.

Iröns, Neville John   *Fans of Imperial China* and *Fans of Imperial Japan*, Hong Kong and London, 1982.

Mayor, Susan   *Collecting Fans*, London, 1980.

Perceval, MacIver   *The Fan Book*, London, 1920.

Rhead, George Wooliscroft   *The History of the Fan*, London, 1910.

Thornton, Peter   'Une des plus belles collections d'éventails du monde' (the Messel Collection), *Connaissance des Arts*, No 134, April, 1963, pp. 93-99.

—Foreword—

BY ANNE, COUNTESS OF ROSSE

That the matchless collection of fans formed by my father, Leonard Messel, finds its lasting home in the Fitzwilliam is my lasting delight. This transfer of responsibility of ownership from family inheritance to a museum in this country, especially to a great university museum, fulfills, I know, my father's wishes, as well as my own. I am very happy that the Friends of the Fitzwilliam, with splendid support from the National Heritage Memorial Fund, should have been able to make this remarkable acquisition possible, keeping together the fans collected for personal delectation, now for the world's students and the fascination of an ever widening circle of the Museum's visitors. I look forward to the day all can see the fans, both Far Eastern and European, installed with the highest professional knowledge and imagination.

My childhood memory carries me back to the years of my father's collecting original fans, ivories and porcelain, when Japanese and Chinese vendors would come to our house in Lancaster Gate from Franck and Co., Camomile Street, during breakfast, to leave him to ponder over the treasures he had suggested looking at, to be discovered later when he came back from the City in the evening. The same applied to representatives from Duvelleroy for his European fans.

It is happy for me that the modern task of cataloguing should be prefaced by this selection of colour plates with an introduction by a friend who has come to know the range of the collection particularly well, Nancy Armstrong, a renowned expert in European fans who this year has been chosen as one of our patrons of the Fan Circle International.

— Introduction —

THE MESSEL-ROSSE COLLECTION OF FANS

The Messel-Rosse Collection of Fans confidently claims its position as the first modern yardstick against which connoisseurs can match their own possessions. In essence it is a teaching collection with its very wide variety of different types of fans, both Oriental and European, and it is the only multi-facetted collection to be seen permanently on view in Europe. It is the personal and private accumulation of one person, Leonard Messel, at the start of the 20th century, exhibiting an enduring aesthetic sensibility and fastidious judgement which anticipated the sophisticated tastes of today.

During the 19th century very few collections of fans were made as they were still in everyday use, yet some *were* put together and subsequently sold at auction as antiques. One such was the Walker Collection Sale; and one most significant collection was eventually deposited at the British Museum, in the late 1880's, by Lady Charlotte Schreiber. Her fans and fan leaves were well researched (the Schreiber Catalogues have been invaluable); they are, however, predominantly printed European examples. As an erudite lady with magpie tendencies (porcelain, lace, fans, playing cards etc.) Lady Charlotte's approach to fans was uplifting: she did not consider them as mere accessories to dress but as thought-provoking art forms, generally with historical or political overtones. One or two French books had been published whilst she was making her collection, charming and poetic, but clearly Lady Charlotte preferred a wider, much more scholarly approach and wished to open up this "new" subject on a more academic level.

During the Art Nouveau period the *avant garde* of Europe became fascinated by the applied arts of Japan, just tentatively emerging after centuries of isolation. Fans were very popular, loosely representing the "mysterious East", and the new styles were readily available in all major cities. They were featured in paintings by the Pre-Raphaelites and the Impressionists, they were fluttered on stage and gaily carried at fancy dress balls.

Taking the lead from both Lady Charlotte and the current trends, both George Wooliscroft Rhead and MacIver Percival then wrote deep, detailed books from 1910-20. These authors covered the fan's progress throughout history from East to West, inspiring connoisseurs to begin making a collection in a quiet and private way: trusted agents, searching for other antiques, would soon find fans added to their shopping lists.

The first fifty years of the 20th century were ones of frenetic pace and change: as a result of the world wars, immense alterations in social habits, classes and dress, fans faded from their established place in everyday use - eventually even from Court appearances.

Just before the books emerged, Leonard Messel started collecting (c. 1905). His fans were never bought for use, nor were they associated in any way with known Messel couture clothes (some of which are at the Museum at Brighton). Their purpose was purely for interest in their rarity and historical background. He appears to have set out to accumulate as many types as he could find, as long as their quality was satisfactory, and above all he exercised his own erudite rule of taste which has perfectly withstood the test of time.

The Messel family were bankers at Darmstadt and personal bankers to the Grand Duke. This banking dynasty decided to establish a branch in England during the 1870s. Leonard Messel (1872-1953), son of Ludwig Messel and Anne Cussans, naturally became a banker too. Educated at Eton and Oxford, he was also thoroughly educated in Fine Arts. He had an inherited love of rare and beautiful things. His father in 1890 had purchased Nymans in Sussex, enlarging the house, and developing the gardens to such an extent that they are of the finest in England: he introduced a rich variety of plants and trees gathered from all over the world. When Leonard Messel inher ited in 1916, not only did he subscribe to many more of the Far Eastern and South American botanical expeditions but he also became an enthusiastic hybridiser. Another of his passionate interests was that in Herbals. His collection ranging from the 13th century was known as the world's finest.

Leonard Messel's London house at Lancaster Gate was palatial, decorated with immense attention to detail in "the Hampton Court" style. He and his wife (Maud Sambourne) considered, for instance, that cushions on chairs were wrong, heavily gilt furniture was vulgar and that all acquisitions should be deeply scholarly and thoroughly researched. They had a splendid library of rare books, the collection of English herbals, a fine collection of antique glass, another of Chinese ivory figures, another of 17th century silver-mounted coconut cups and yet another of fans. Tragically one snowy night in February 1947 Nymans was burnt to the ground, turning the collection of Herbals to powder: fortunately the fan collection was at Lancaster Gate but unhappily the catalogues and relevant papers all went up in flames. Luckily Eleanor Sinclair Rhode had spent almost two years recording the Herbals, but the loss of the fan catalogues has occasioned much recent research.

Leonard Messel's daughter, Anne (1902) married twice; firstly the barrister Ronald Armstrong-Jones and secondly, in 1935, Michael, 6th Earl of Rosse. She had two children from each marriage. Her partnership with Lord Rosse became historic as they stimulated each other, especially in their many fields of preservation, and Lady Rosse has felt endlessly inspired by her husband all her life.

The Rosse family homes are Birr Castle in Eire and Womersley Park in Yorkshire. Lady Rosse also inherited from her mother No 18 Stafford Terrace in London which had originally been built for her maternal grandfather, Edward Linley Sambourne (1844-1910), the political cartoonist and illustrator who took over from Sir John Tenniel at *Punch*. Then, from her parents, Lady Rosse inherited Nymans. Recently, having most lovingly and carefully conserved both these properties with her husband, she has seen them passed on to the right hands: the Greater London Council now has Stafford Terrace as a London museum and the National Trust administers the gardens of Nymans. Lady Rosse remains a Director of the latter, ceaselessly at work.

Leonard Messel left his collection of fans to his daughter Anne, grateful for her and her husband's selfless help after the fire and aware that she was dedicated to conservation and preservation. So the fans have remained wrapped individually in acid-free tissue paper, housed in the dark of long, shallow drawers, away from inexpert fingers and adverse conditions.

Lady Rosse was persuaded to put certain of her fans on exhibition at the Victoria and Albert Museum in 1963. The exhibition was a brilliant success, much interest was aroused, and a glimmer of new light dawned in academic fields. Sadly no illustrated catalogue was issued and we had to wait until 1974 for the first of the new books on fans. When this emerged a few owners of fans immediately became avid for further information and at once began to accumulate anything they saw. Some of them bought a generalised collection and some specialised, collecting French fans, or lace or ivory ones; some saw fans purely as costume accessories and others wished to collect entirely from a social history standpoint. The newly published books were required to show as many coloured illustrations as feasible, for identification purposes, for there was nowhere where a large collection of fans could be seen and studied on a regular basis without prior arrangements, or where East might be compared with West. Also not all auction house catalogues were absolutely accurate, and some dealers' assertions left much to be desired.

A new collecting society, the Fan Circle International (now a registered charity), greatly helped the new-born study of fans by producing written matter in the thrice yearly *Bulletin*, and by mounting specialist exhibitions. They chose the Countess of Rosse to be one of their most prestigious Patrons because of her custody of the Messel Collection, and have been especially grateful for her loving concern towards the society. Just recently the Fan Association of North America (FANA) has also been formed, and the fan is now being featured annually in specialist exhibitions worldwide. Suddenly the fan has "arrived", and the prices at auction have risen astronomically.

It is a momentous event that such a famous University museum should decide to acquire (through the Friends of the Fitzwilliam and the National Heritage Memorial Fund) the Messel-Rosse fans for their academic content and not just as an adjunct to costume. The authorities have recognised that Leonard Messel collected as a cool purist with no thought of re-selling, refusing to bow to "flash and cash" and used quality as his yardstick. Each fan is here on its own merits.

The unique seventeenth century standing feather fan (illus.1) is now considered a national treasure, recalling imports from the East India Company, very rare and fragile. The c.1665 fan (illus.2), made from transparent mica panels, delicately painted, is one of only four presently known in the world. The splendid painted fan showing "The Expulsion of Heliodorus from the Temple" is a pastiche of Solimena's fresco in the Gesù Nuovo at Naples of 1725 (illus.12). The iridescent silver sequinned one (not illustrated) brings us right up to the jazz age of the 1920's. Some of the printed political fans deserve study by social historians, some of the China trade fans are the earliest known in Europe, and the English fan (illus.14) showing Mrs Fitzherbert and the Prince Regent (after Cosway) reconciles technical ability with feminine enchantment. Two fans seem especially reminiscent of both Anne Rosse and Leonard Messel with their wonderful work at Nymans Gardens - both are printed fans, one (illus.6) showing Fair Rosamond in a formal garden with Woodstock Palace in the background, the other (illus. 16) printed by Sarah Ashton with delicate botanical details and lines from Erasmus Darwin's *The Botanic Garden*.

There are a number of chinoiserie fans, up to every trick in the book, with hidden scenes or differing techniques. Chinoiserie attributions are tantalisingly difficult: in the field of ceramics, for instance, we first had Germany copying the Orient, Britain then copying Germany, and then the Orient copying the British copies of the German copies of the Orient. With no distinguishing marks chinoiserie fans may be from any stable, yet certain types soon became apparent, especially in stylish France. The Chinese never made fans from skins (vellum, kid or chickenskin), always used a brush (Europeans sometimes used spattering pens), and they considered heavy gilding rather vulgar. The Germans very much enjoyed the Chinese decorative arts but "clobbered" them with gold to suit their own tastes. Special chinoiserie fans worth studying are the black, white and rose-coloured fan after Pillement (illus.29), which has been much published; the China trade fan showing a visitor from Brazil meeting a Braganza Princess (illus.32), and the "House of the Courtesans" fan, (illus.28). This one is astonishing in its state of preservation with its mica "windows" and lavishly applied straw work.

Dating a fan can be as difficult as deciding its country of origin. Consider, if you will, some Chinese sticks and guards which have been exported from Amoy, by junk and galleon, via the Philippines to Antwerp, whilst a fine kid leaf is painted in Vienna. Finally assembled in Amsterdam that fan may be sold in Stockholm, Madrid or London with the assembling fan seller's name on the box. What, then, is its origin?

Clearly many are an amalgam.

Broadly speaking Leonard Messel collected an (almost) equal number of European fans from France, England, Spain, the Italian States, the Germanic countries and the North-West of Europe. From a variety of countries he made a selection of horn fans, ivory brisé ones, textile fans, and printed ones as well as the chinoiserie fans mentioned above. There are fans of vellum, kid, chickenskin, paper and silk; embroidered painted, printed and decorated, using threads, straw, gut, mica, plaques of mother-of-pearl, feathers, spangles, paillettes and sequins. The sticks and guards are of every material known, and crafted with every technique. The equally large Oriental section of the collection stretches across a huge area of land and encompasses many different backgrounds. There are fans from China, Japan, India, Indonesia and Korea. Some are fixed or rigid in their construction, such as the pair of mica temple fans (illus.37), others are folding, painted in delicate watercolours (illus.49) and yet others are brisé, such as the lacquered ivory one (illus.34) from Japan, with its taka-makie-e and hiramaki-e work, and shibayama-style inlay on the guards. The virtue of the Oriental section, as in the European one, is its range of subject matter and types.

There are many fans from Japan, from the brutal weapons of war (illus.51) made of iron, to the poetic ink and opaque watercolours of Toyomaro (not illustrated) showing a girl with an umbrella c.1795. Even though the Japanese enthused about cherry blossom they also sighed with a deep sense of lost youth and time passing, often making expeditions in the autumn to admire withered grasses.

Many of the fans remain unmounted or have been dismounted, regarded as too precious to use but admired for their painterly qualities. One of Lady Rosse's favourite stories told to her by her father is to be seen on the fan illustrating a "Hare gazing at the Autumn Moon" (illus.49), recalling the legend of the hare who lives in the moon, pounding the drug of immortality.

In Chinese mythology the festival of the Moon is one of the three great annual Chinese feasts, and takes place on the fifteenth day of the eighth month, at the full moon of the autumn equinox. The Moon is said to be inhabited by a personage who is considered the Moon goddess, Ch'ang-o. She is the wife of I the Excellent Archer, a mythological personage who brought down nine suns with his arrows, one day when the ten suns of primitive times took it into their heads to rise together and threaten to shrivel up the world. The gods had given him the drug of immortality and one day he returned home to find his wife had eaten it. He was so angry that she fled to the Moon, her husband in hot pursuit. She asked protection of the Hare who fought with I and made him give up his intention of punishing his wife, who henceforth has lived in the Moon. The couple were later reconciled, however, and I would visit her in her lunar palace. She is always represented as a beautiful woman, and her name is often mentioned in novels and poems for it is said currently of a pretty woman that she is as "beautiful as if Ch'ang-o had come down from the moon".

The Messel Collection of fans is to be known as the Messel-Rosse Collection because Lady Rosse carried out her instructions learned at her father's knee since childhood. Encouraged by her enlightened husband she had let them lie quietly, generously lending them now and again for exhibitions, allowing hardly anyone to handle them, giving none away as impulsive presents and resisting the temptation to add to them by buying more at auction house sales.

It is fitting that one of her oldest and dearest friends (and an Eton friend of Lord Rosse) should have the final word. Sir Harold Acton has written from Florence:

"In this air-conditioned age the cooling fan has almost disappeared. A sad loss to polite society, for a fan could also accentuate wit and puncture indiscretion. We seldom, if ever, see one as in the drawingroom of Lady Windermere, whose fan was the subject of a delightful comedy. In fact I know of only one lady of quality who could *flirt* a fan - I believe that is the correct term - with proper elegance and grace. I refer to Anne, Countess of Rosse, the wittiest of mortals, who has now surrendered her father's unique collection of these exquisite instruments to the Fitzwilliam Museum at Cambridge. Even if these can no longer be flirted by the fair, they will enchant the beholder with their variety of form and design. What a Lucullan feast for weary eyes! All praise to the generous heiress of these rarities who has resisted the lucrative offers to dispose of them abroad."

Nancy Armstrong.

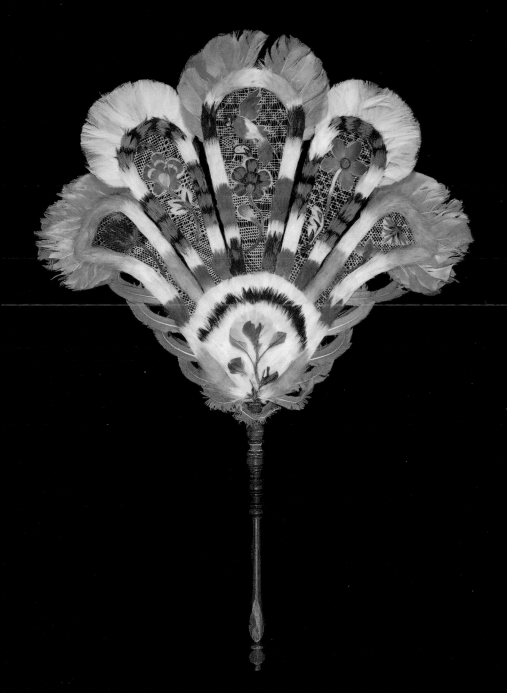

1 The *Messel Feather Fan*. English or Dutch, 17th century.

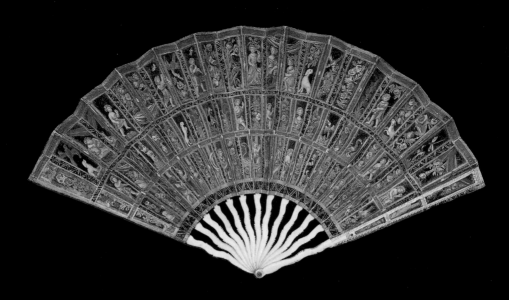

2 *The Mica Fan.* c. 1665.

3 Italian folding fan. c. 1680–1720.

4 *Aurora and Cephalus*, after Annibale Caracci. Italian.
c. 1750-80.

5 *Perseus and Andromeda*, after Annibale Caracci. Italian.
c. 1760.

6 *The Fair Rosamond fan*. English. 1740.

7 Detail of the above.

8 Silk Court fan. French. c. 1760.

9 Rococo folding fan, probably French. c. 1770.

10 *The Billiards fan*. Venetian. c. 1730.

11 English folding fan. c. 1780.

12 The Expulsion of Heliodorus Fan, after Solimena. 1725.

13 Detail of the above. The sticks and guards are later.

14 The *Mrs Fitzherbert Fan*. English. c. 1785.

15 Detail of Mrs Fitzherbert and the Prince Regent.

16 *The Botanical Fan*. English. 1792.

17 An "Assignat" fan. French. 1792.

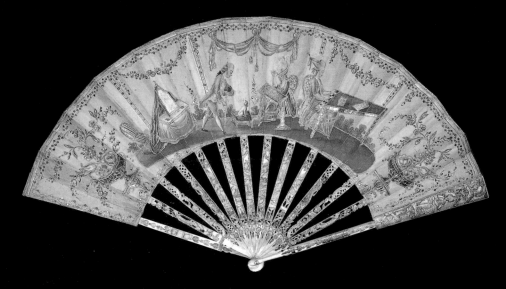

18 Silk Court fan. French. c. 1770.

19 Detail of the above.

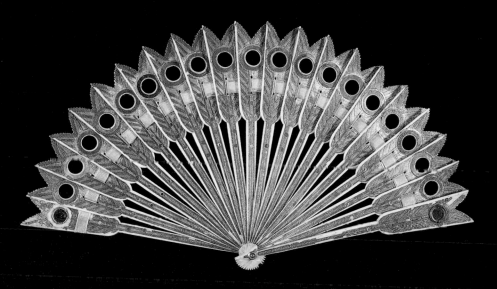

20 Tiny lorgnette fan - *Love's arrows*. c. 1790.

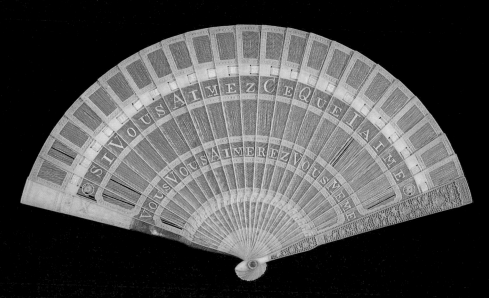

21 Tiny French brisé fan. c. 1790–1820.

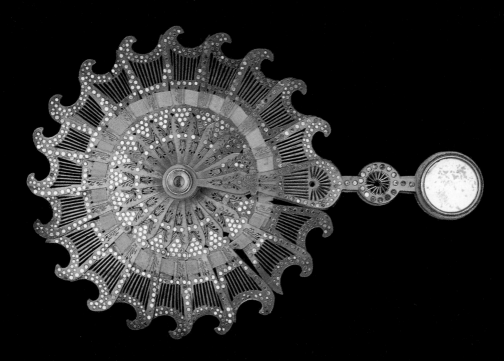

22 Horn cockade quizzing fan. c. 1790-1810.

23 *The Coronation of Napoleon Fan* after J. L. David. c. 1807.

24 Spanish marriage fan. c. 1830.

25 *The Corradino Dance Fan.* c. 1830.

26 Multi-ribboned horn fan. c. 1810.

27 Brisé "Three Scenes" fan. French. c. 1780.

28 *The House of the Courtesans Fan*. c. 1750.

29 Chinoiserie fan, after Pillement. c. 1750.

30 Chinoiserie "Four Scenes" fan. c. 1770.

31 An "Applied Faces" fan. c. 1850.

32 *The Braganza Fan.* c. 1807.

33 German chinoiserie fan. c. 1750.

34 Japanese ivory brisé lacquered fan. c. 1860.

35 Early Chinese trade fan. c. 1680–1720.

36 Korea: Fixed Fan (Pu-ch'ae), for shaman dancing, with the
triple jewel (T'aeguk) design; 19th century.

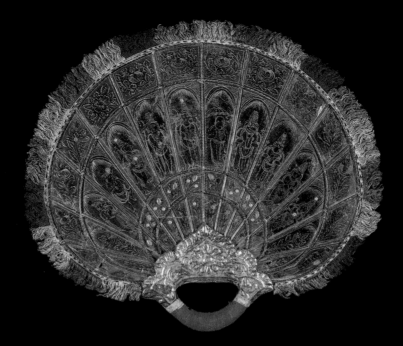

37 South India: Fixed Fan for temple use, with Hindu deities.
19th century.

38 Japan: Folding Fan (Gunsen) for use in battle, with sun and
moon disks. 18th century.

39 Japan: Heron and lotus. Kano school. 18th century.

40 Japan: Phoenix and paulownia. Kano school. 18th century.

41 Japan: Sparrow on snowy bamboo. Sotatsu style.
18th century.

42 Japan: Puppies, bamboo and stream. Rimpa style.
17th century.

43 Japan: Hoopoe, peony and iris. Kano school. 18th century.

44 Japan: Tiger and bamboo. Signed: Kyūzan (b. 1863). Late
19th century.

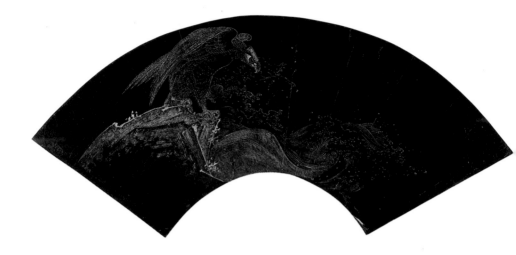

45 Japan: Sea eagle. Kano school. 18th century.

46 Japan: Eagle attacking a duck. Kano school. 18th century.

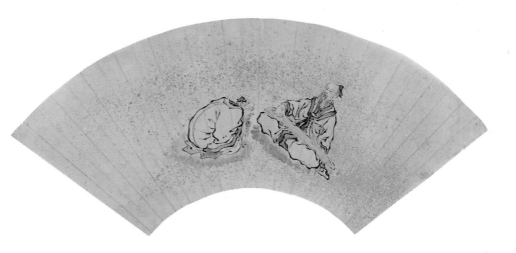

47 Japan: Two scholars in antique Chinese Costume. Kano school. 18th/19th century.

48 Japan: The Seven Sages of the Bamboo Grove. Kano school. 18th century.

49 Japan: Moon-gazing hare and autumn plants. Shijo school.
19th century.

50 Japan: Mounted Mongol hunting rabbits. Kano school.
18th century

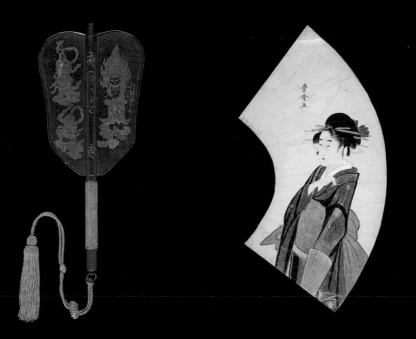

Japan: *Left* 51 Screen Fan (Gampai Uchiwa) for signalling in battle. Probably 17th century. *Right* 52 Girl holding an umbrella. Ukiyo-e school. Signed: Toyomaro. c. 1795.

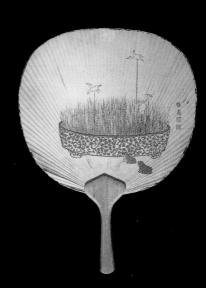

Japan: *Left* 53 Screen Fan (Uchiwa) with *chidori* over waves at sunset. Ukiyo-e school: Signed: Samori or Sae. Dated 1861. *Right* 54 Screen Fan with model frogs, jardinière with shoots and model cranes. Signed: Gakyo (or Masataka). 19th century.

55 Japan: Top-class prostitute (Oiran) and attendants on parade.
Ukiyo-e school. Signed: Hokuba (1779-1844). c. 1830-40.

56 Japan: Girl on a verandah from the series "Seven Modern
Laughing Women". Ukiyo-e school. Signed: Ichiyūsai Kuniyoshi.
Dated 1847/8.

絹甫大兄
清拂
弟餘慶

57 China: Screen Fan, with kingfisher on flowering lotus.
Signed, with a dedication, by Yuqing. Qing dynasty, 18th/19th
century. The artist's name was hereditary in the Li family.

58 China: Butterflies among flowering plants. Signed, with a
poem, by Yun Bing (fl. 1670-1710). c. 1700.

59 China: Sparrow and grasshopper on pine tree. Signed Kuei
Fang. Dated probably equivalent to 1811.

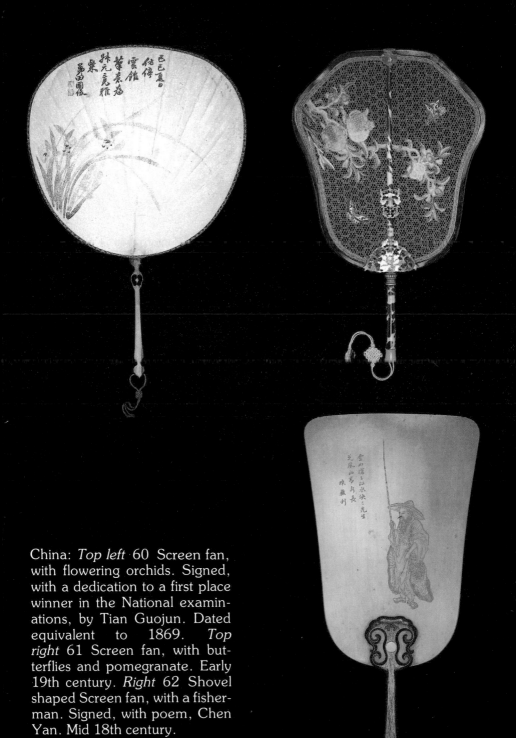

China: *Top left* 60 Screen fan, with flowering orchids. Signed, with a dedication to a first place winner in the National examinations, by Tian Guojun. Dated equivalent to 1869. *Top right* 61 Screen fan, with butterflies and pomegranate. Early 19th century. *Right* 62 Shovel shaped Screen fan, with a fisherman. Signed, with poem, Chen Yan. Mid 18th century.

63 China: Screen Fan ("mandarin" type), with cockatoo and
peonies. Mid-late 19th century.